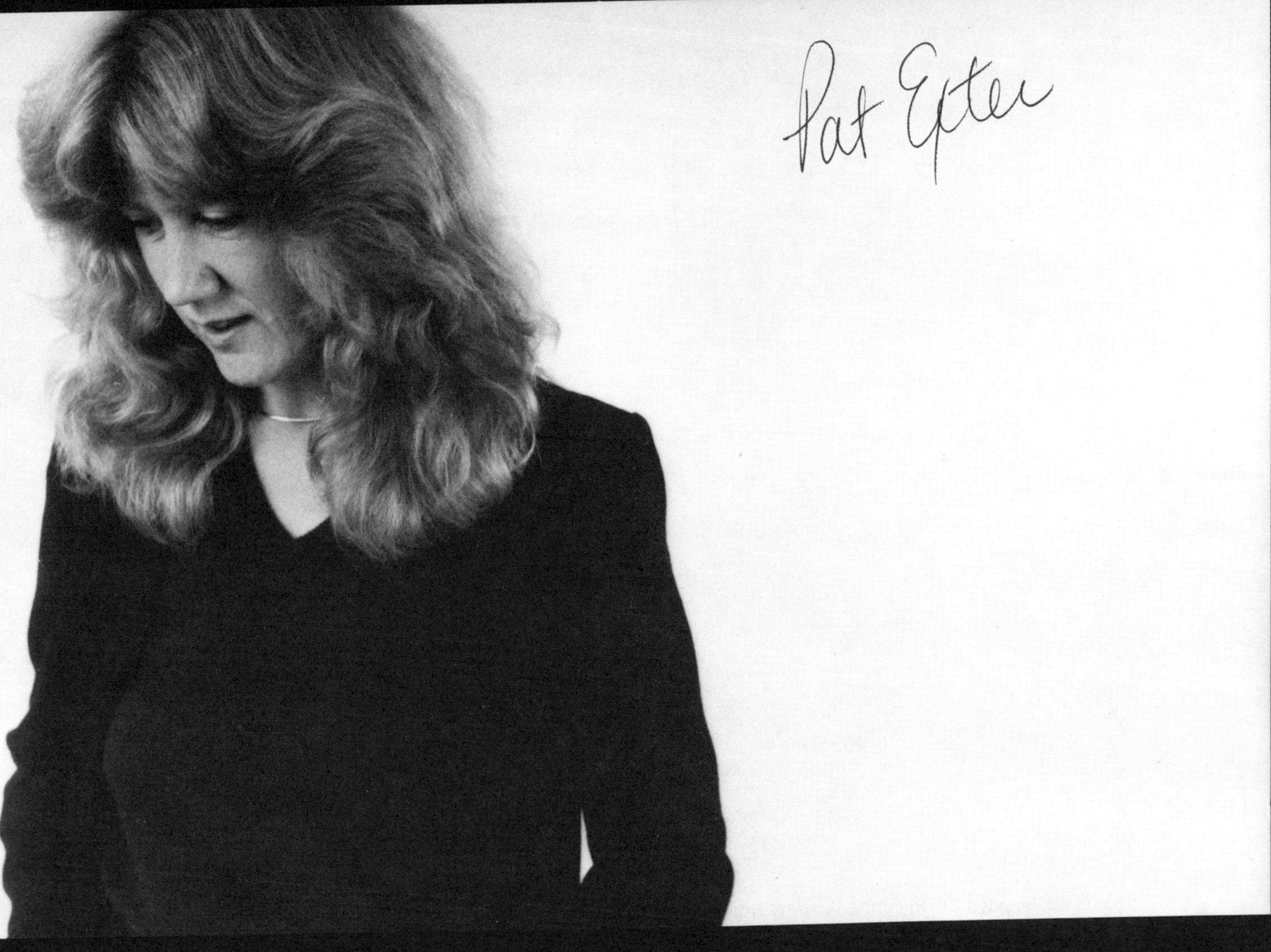

Singing For Our Lives
By Holly Near

Published By Redwood Records
Oakland, California

Compiled by Jo-Lynne Worley, Adrienne Torf, Holly Near and Joanie Shoemaker.
Designed by Cathy McAuliffe
Cover Photo by Irene Young
Typeset by The Typesetting Shop, Oakland, CA
Musical typesetting by Paulette Claver, Musica Engraving, Concord, CA.
Guitar Chord Chart by Mimi Fox and Lisa MacGregor
Printed in the United States by BookCrafters, Inc., Michigan

ISBN 0-9608774-2-8
All rights reserved. No part of this book may be reproduced
in any form without permission in writing from the publisher.

Copyright © 1982, Hereford Music
476 West MacArthur Boulevard
Oakland, CA 94609

Distributed by Redwood Records
476 West MacArthur Boulevard
Oakland, CA 94609

CONTENTS

- 4 Introduction
- 6 Ain't No Where You Can Run
- 8 Fight Back
- 10 Fire In The Rain
- 12 Foolish Notion
- 14 Golden Thread
- 17 Hay Una Mujer
- 19 I Got Trouble
- 20 Imagine My Surprise
- 23 Kentucky Woman
- 25 Mountain Song
- 26 Lady At The Piano
- 29 Nina
- 31 No Loss Of Pride
- 32 Once Or Twice
- 34 Put Away
- 36 Riverboat
- 38 Rock Me In Your Arms
- 39 The Rock Will Wear Away
- 41 Singing For Our Lives
- 42 Sit With Me
- 45 Something About The Women
- 47 Take It With You
- 49 Voices
- 50 Warnings
- 52 Working Woman
- 56 Wrap the Sun Around You
- 60 You Bet
- 64 Chord Explanation
- 65 Chord Chart
- 67 Notes

Irene Young

INTRODUCTION

1982, the year of this printing, marks the ten year anniversary of Redwood Records. We are happy and proud to have reached our ten year mark — to have grown with Holly through her musical development and to have worked with many fine musicians, groups, organizations, producers, distributors, sponsors, and individuals along the way. Our audiences have been very loyal, supportive, and constantly asking for lyrics and sheet music. Out of the celebration of our ten year anniversary we bring you **Singing For Our Lives.** Recorded versions of most of the songs in this book can be found on Holly Near's albums, **Imagine My Surprise** and **Fire In The Rain.**

The first collection, **Words and Music,** is a special edition that represents the first five years of Redwood's existence. Recorded versions of those songs can be found on **Hang In There, A Live Album,** and **You Can Know All I Am** by Holly Near.

Due to the constant state of change and growth in our minds, our lives and our company, certain parts of this book feel dated to us, but for historic purposes we have left them as is.

Our warm thanks to Adrienne Torf for her coordination of the work on this book.

Enjoy!

Redwood Records

Ain't Nowhere You Can Run

Words and Music by
HOLLY NEAR

Anti-nuke demonstration, Denver, 1979

Ain't Nowhere You Can Run—2

Fight Back

Best heard when sung by thousands.

Words and Music by
HOLLY NEAR

Copyright 1978 Hereford Music

This song was originally written a cappella. Chords as they appear here are by Adrienne Torf.

Fire In The Rain

Words and Music by
HOLLY NEAR

Foolish Notion

Words and Music by
HOLLY NEAR

CODA

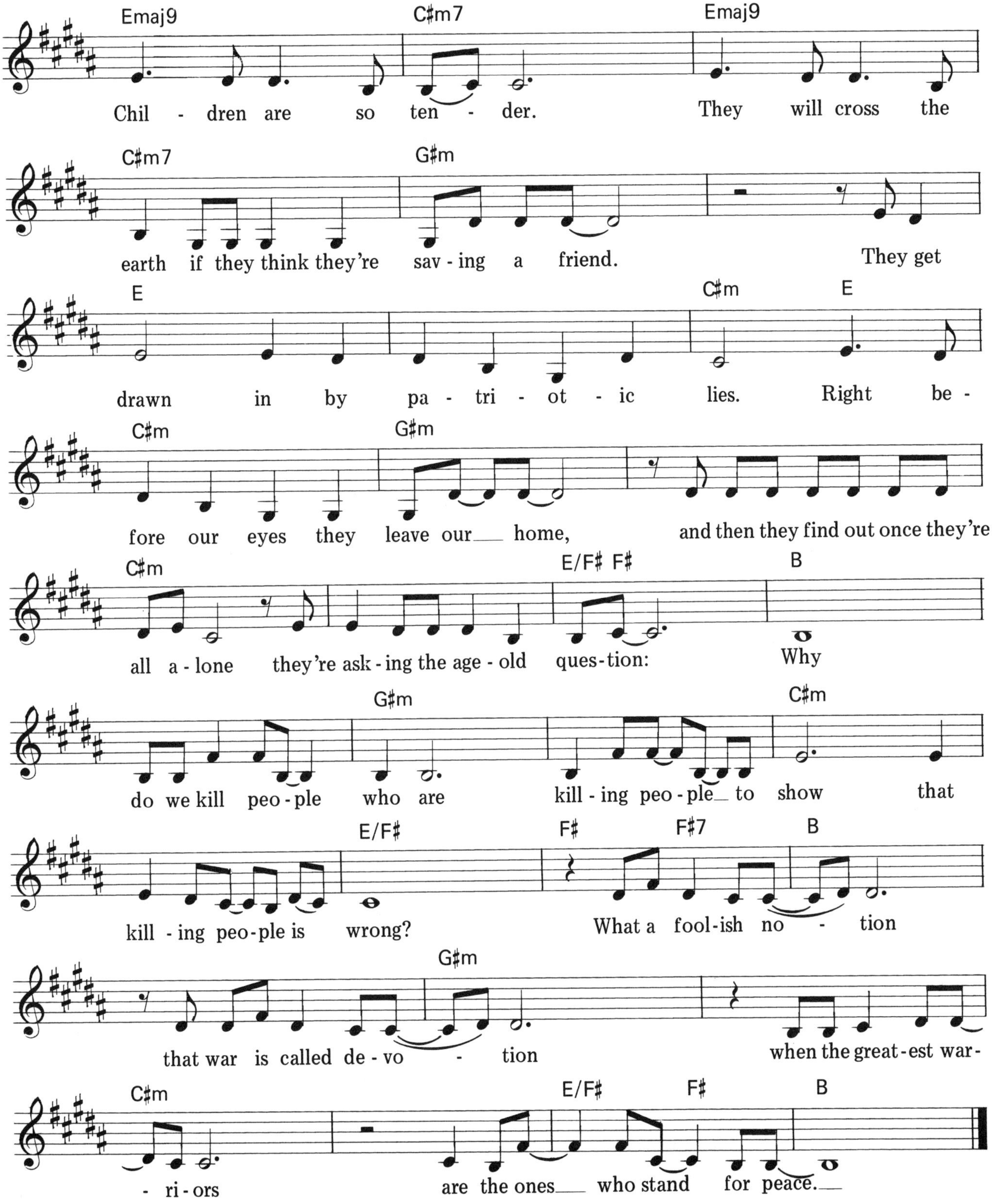

Emaj9 C♯m7 Emaj9
Chil - dren are so ten - der. They will cross the
C♯m7 G♯m
earth if they think they're sav - ing a friend. They get
E C♯m E
drawn in by pa - tri - ot - ic lies. Right be -
C♯m G♯m
fore our eyes they leave our home, and then they find out once they're
C♯m E/F♯ F♯ B
all a - lone they're ask - ing the age - old ques - tion: Why
G♯m C♯m
do we kill peo - ple who are kill - ing peo - ple to show that
E/F♯ F♯ F♯7 B
kill - ing peo - ple is wrong? What a fool - ish no - tion
G♯m
that war is called de - vo - tion when the great - est war -
C♯m E/F♯ F♯ B
- ri - ors are the ones who stand for peace.

Chord Explanations:

Emaj9
C♯m7

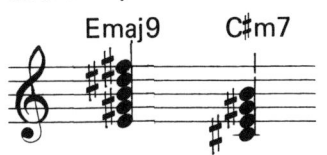

Hay Una Mujer

Words and Music by
HOLLY NEAR

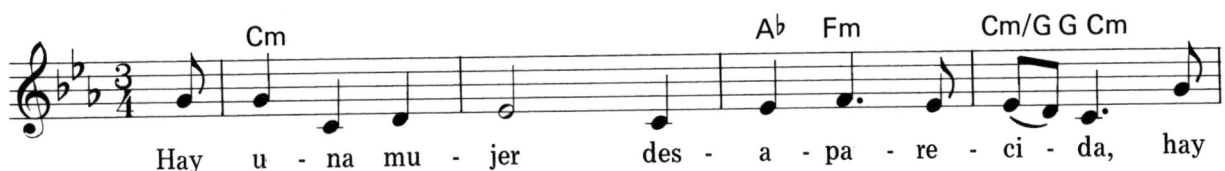

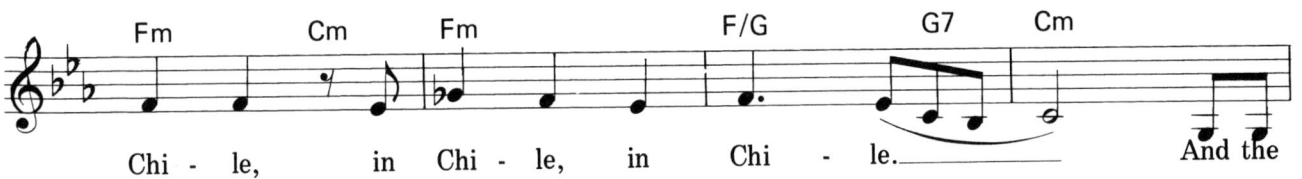

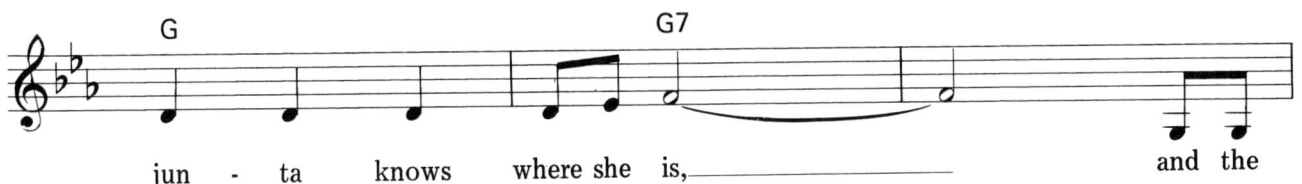
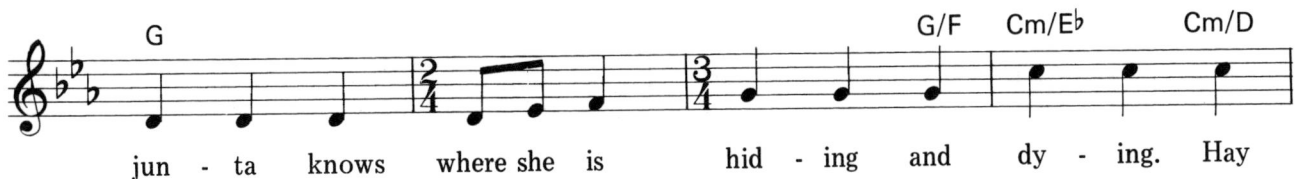

Copyright 1978 Hereford Music

On September 11, 1973 a military coup overthrew the democratically elected socialist government of Salvador Allende. 2000 people were killed, over 7000 detained in The Stadium, and all human and civil rights suspended. Since then over 900 political prisoners have "disappeared". Due to the courage of the Chilean people, popular resistance to the military junta has survived and grown.

(I Got) Trouble

Words and Music by
HOLLY NEAR

I've been laid off, trouble, got trouble. I've been laid off, trouble tonight.

First I want to talk about it. Then I want to fight. Then I want to make love to you all night.

I've been laid off, trouble, got trouble. I've been laid off, trouble tonight.

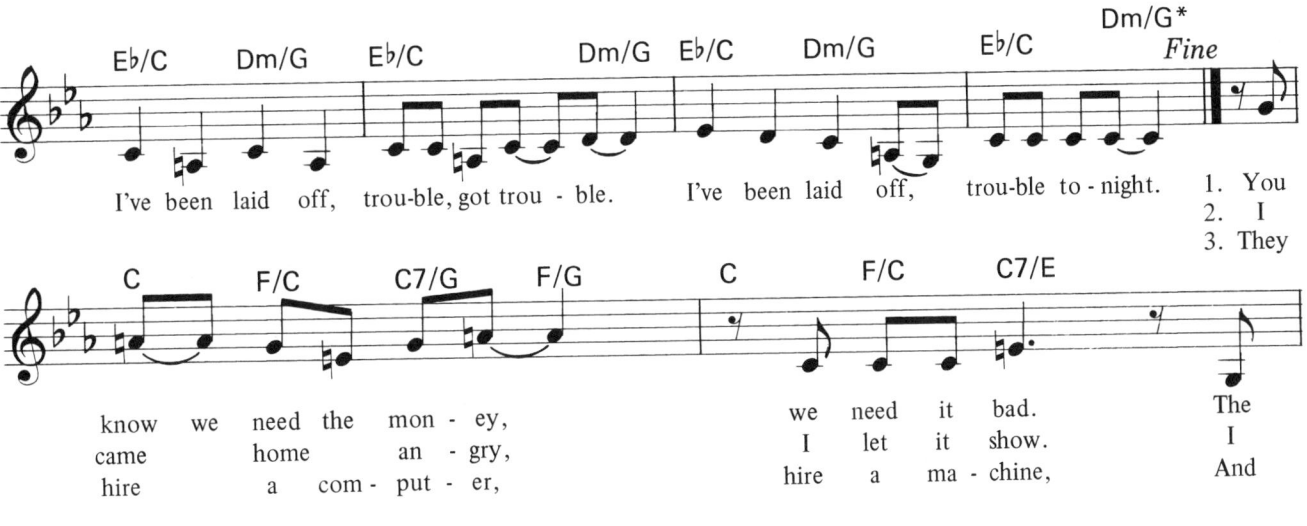

1. You know we need the money, we need it bad. The
2. I came home angry, I let it show. I
3. They hire a computer, hire a machine, And

money I was making is the last that we had to do the
didn't mean to blame it on the best friend I know. I love you,
then they call the product the "American Dream." And it ain't

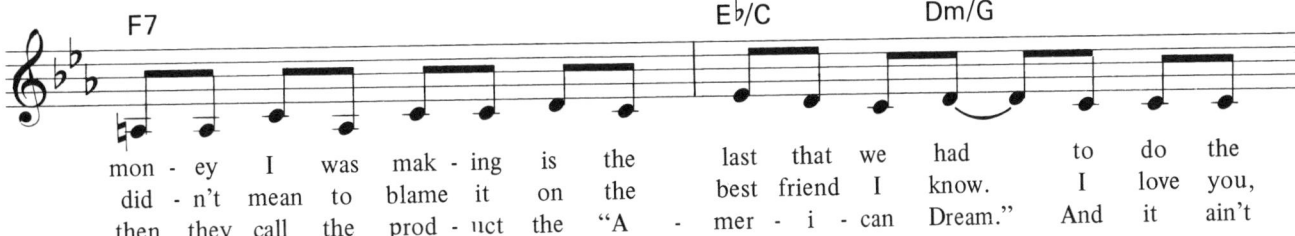

feeding, feeding. Our kids need clothes. Feeding, feeding. Payment on the loan.
darlin', darlin'. Let's sleep in late. Come tomorrow, I'll go out and agitate.
working, working. It's no surprise. When you ain't working, time to organize.

*Omit last time.   Copyright 1981 Hereford Music

"This is a new lyric to an old song. The original version can be found on **A Live Album** where it is titled 'Laid Off' and is also available in the **Words and Music** Songbook. I re-wrote the lyrics because I wanted to see if the heroine could get angry and active rather than be a victim of circumstance. I think she did fine!"- HN

Imagine My Surprise!

Words and Music by HOLLY NEAR

Imagine my surprise! I love that I have found you, But I ache all over wanting to know your every dream. Imagine my surprise! to find that I love you, Feeling warm all over knowing that you've been alive. Pirates off an eastern coast, women you lived in danger; but I hear your laughter, free of petticoats. No need for foolish chivalry though you're living in the eighteenth century. You make love to each other on your boats out on the sea. Imagine my surprise! I

Copyright 1978 Hereford Music

In history class we mainly memorized the names of kings, presidents, and wars. " 'Where is your Shakespeare?' 'She was a lesbian and you burned her books.' " © 1976 Women's Graphic Collective

Kentucky Woman

Words and Music by
HOLLY NEAR

Copyright 1978 Hereford Music

Mountain Song

Words and Music by
HOLLY NEAR

Copyright 1978 Hereford Music

Timothy Near

"Sometimes you can't tell by just looking!"

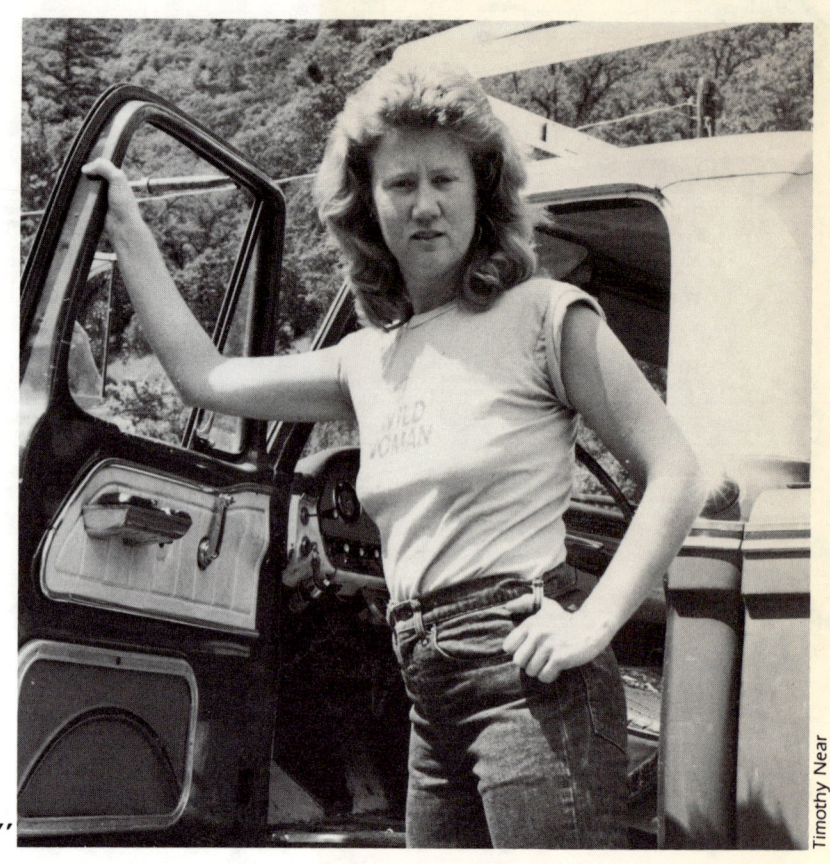

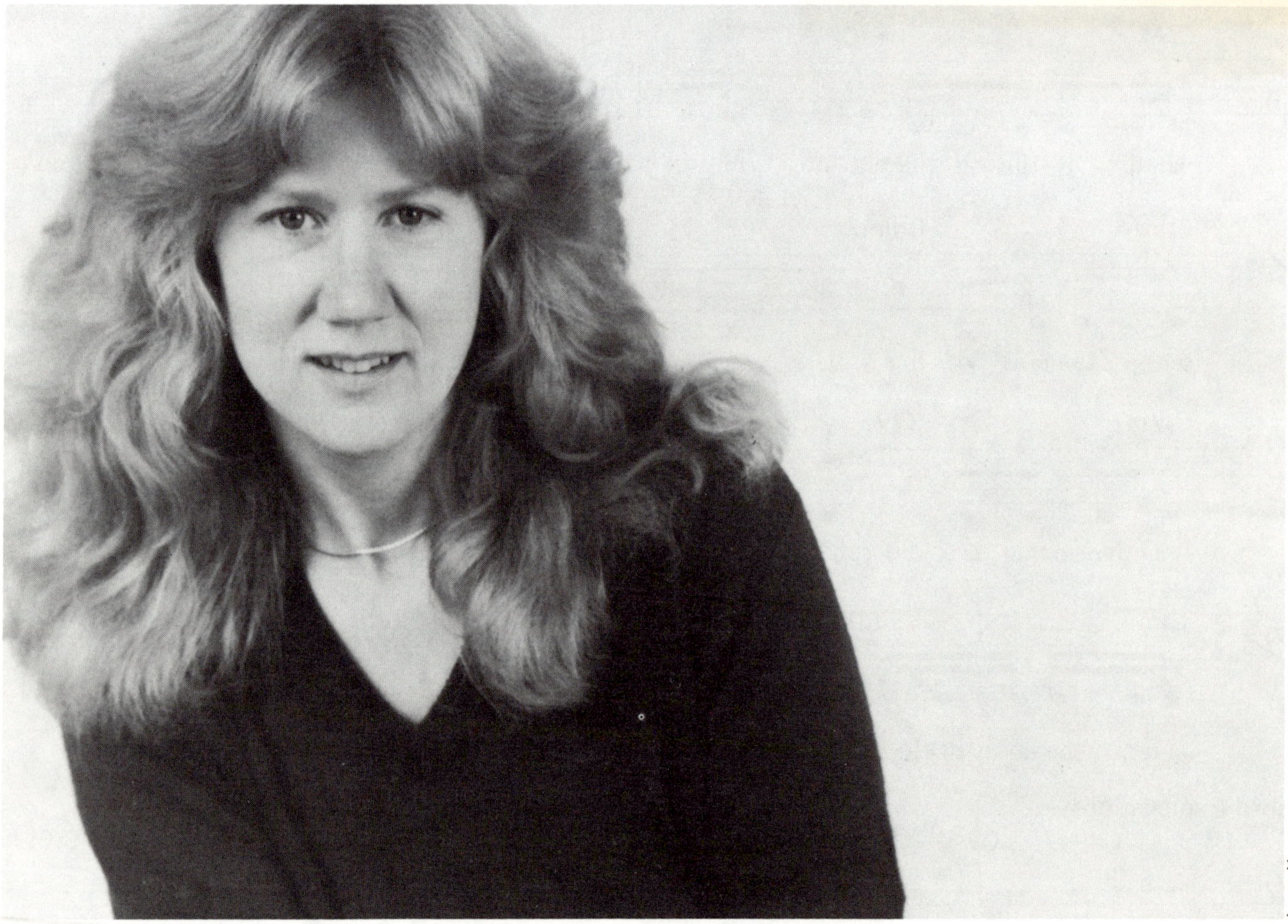

Irene Young

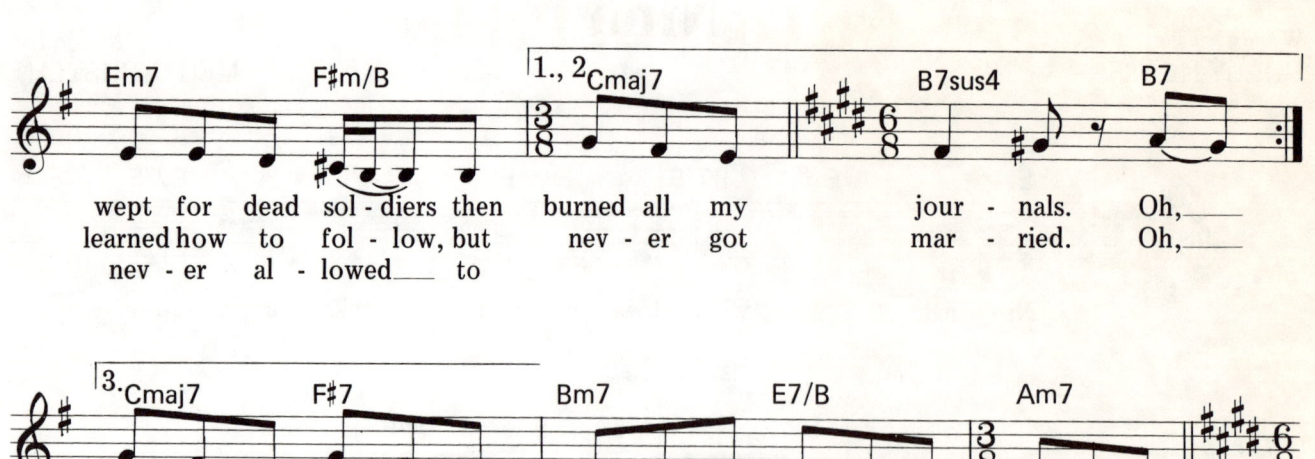

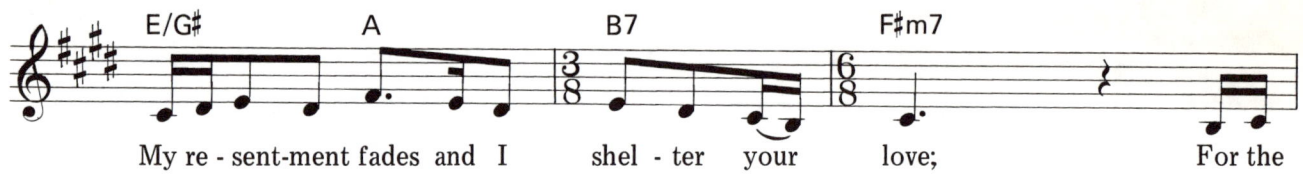

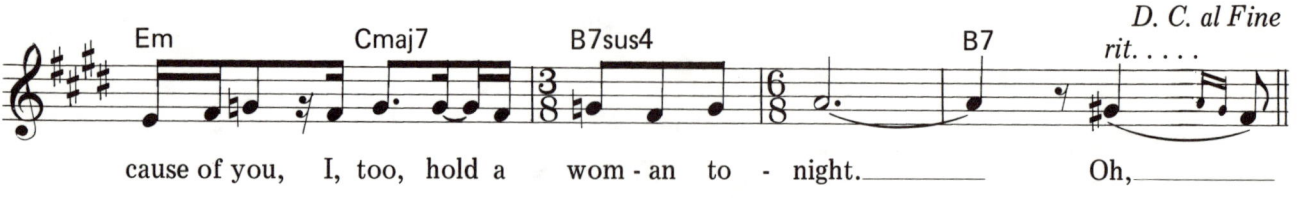

Chord Explanations:

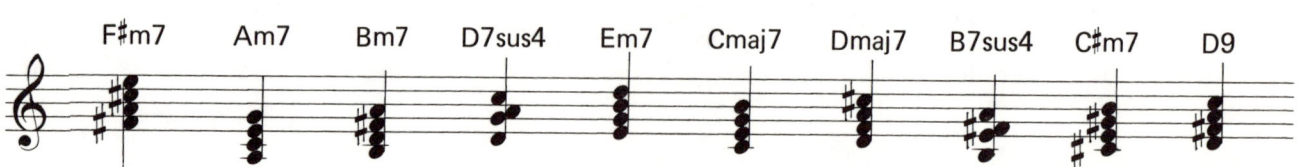

No Loss Of Pride

Words and Music by
HOLLY NEAR

Copyright 1981 Hereford Music

Once Or Twice

Words and Music by
HOLLY NEAR

Sometimes you say a look will cross my eye
while we're sit - ting close to touch and talk - ing,
like my brain is say - ing, "Don't go it all the way.
Save that kind of feel - ing for an - oth - er day." Oh,
that kind of lov - ing can make a trav - el - er stay.

Sometimes you say a look will cross my eye
while I sit a - lone and you are play - ing,
like my heart is say - ing, "Don't play that song to - day,
Not while I'm try - ing to pack and get on my way." Oh,
that kind of mu - sic can make a fid - dl - er stay.

I guess I could get up, and I would walk right out the door.

Copyright 1981 Hereford Music

Once Or Twice—2

Riverboat

Words and Music by
HOLLY NEAR

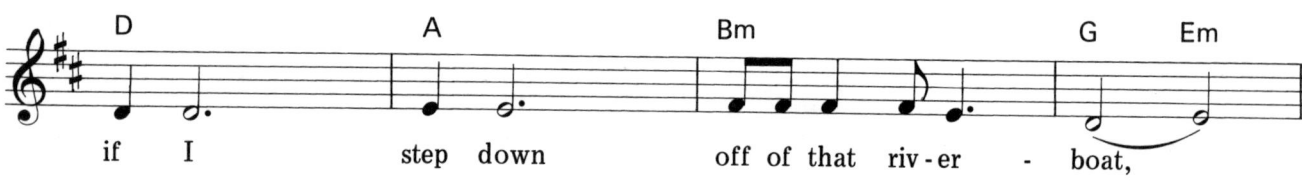

Copyright 1978 Hereford Music

Riverboat—2

The Rock Will Wear Away

Words by
HOLLY NEAR

Music by
MEG CHRISTIAN

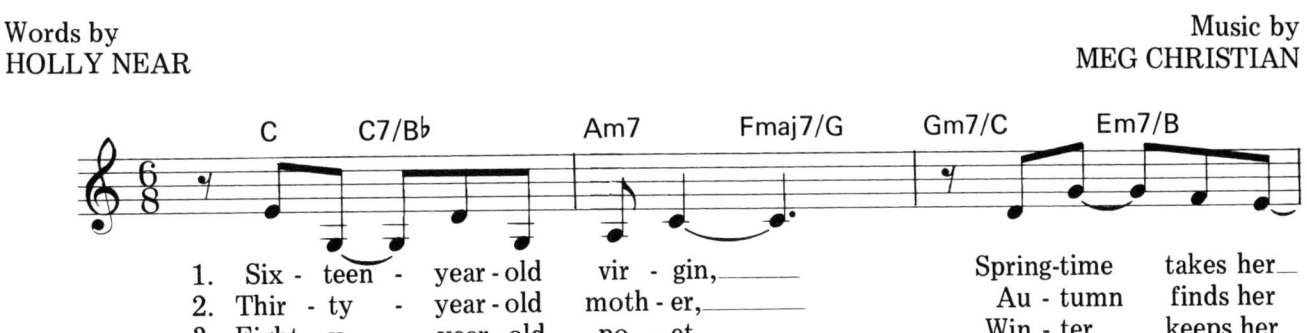

1. Six - teen - year - old vir - gin, Spring-time takes her
2. Thir - ty - year - old moth - er, Au - tumn finds her
3. Eight - y - year - old po - et, Win - ter keeps her

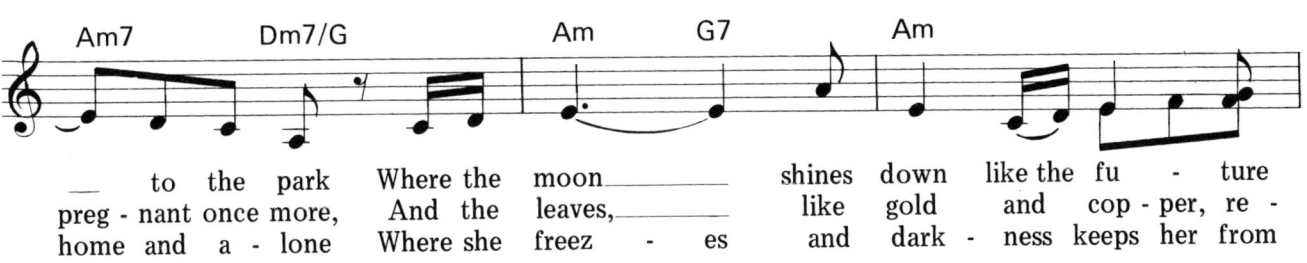

— to the park Where the moon shines down like the fu - ture
preg - nant once more, And the leaves, like gold and cop - per, re -
home and a - lone Where she freez - es and dark - ness keeps her from

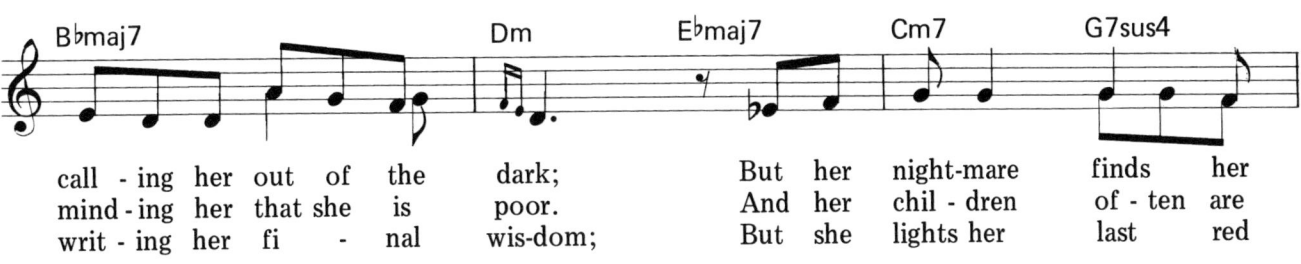

call - ing her out of the dark; But her night-mare finds her
mind - ing her that she is poor. And her chil - dren of - ten are
writ - ing her fi - nal wis-dom; But she lights her last red

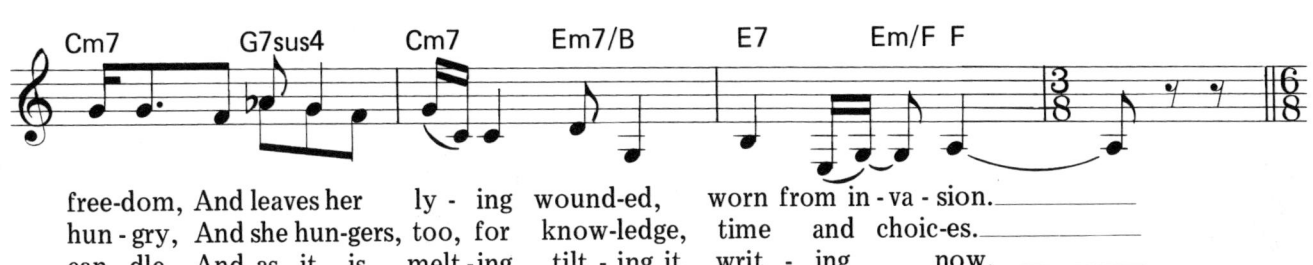

free - dom, And leaves her ly - ing wound-ed, worn from in - va - sion.
hun - gry, And she hun - gers, too, for know - ledge, time and choic - es.
can - dle, And as it is melt - ing, tilt - ing it, writ - ing now.

Copyright 1977 Hereford Music/Thumbelina Music

40　The Rock Will Wear Away—2

Singing For Our Lives

Words and Music by
HOLLY NEAR

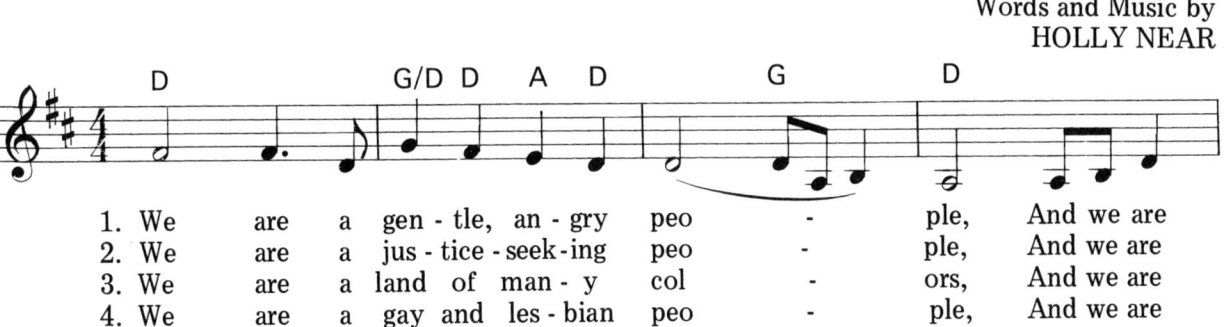

1. We are a gen-tle, an-gry peo - ple, And we are
2. We are a jus-tice-seek-ing peo - ple, And we are
3. We are a land of man-y col - ors, And we are
4. We are a gay and les-bian peo - ple, And we are

sing - ing, sing - ing for our lives.
sing - ing, sing - ing for our lives.
sing - ing, sing - ing for our lives.
sing - ing, sing - ing for our lives.

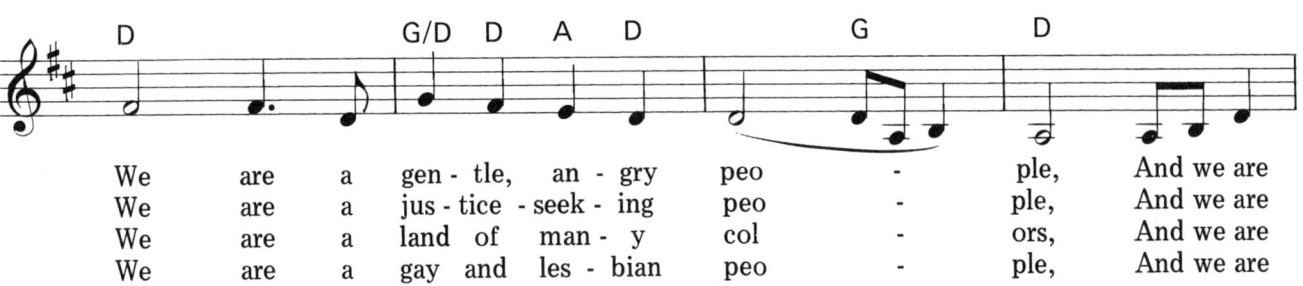

We are a gen-tle, an-gry peo - ple, And we are
We are a jus-tice-seek-ing peo - ple, And we are
We are a land of man-y col - ors, And we are
We are a gay and les-bian peo - ple, And we are

sing - ing, sing - ing for our lives.
sing - ing, sing - ing for our lives.
sing - ing, sing - ing for our lives.
sing - ing, sing - ing for our lives.

Copyright 1979 Hereford Music

1. Am/D … Dm/G
lay be-side me, hold me while I cry.

2. Am/D   Dm/G   B♭/C
not in me, my friend, to ac-cept de - feat.   So won't you please

Am/F   Em/A
sit with me   through the night,   and tell me it's

Am/D   Dm   Gm   B♭/G   B♭/C   C
all right   to fall a-part   with   you.

B♭/G   Am/D
Find-ing a friend in you   to wake me in the morn-ing,

B♭/G   Cm   E♭/C
Find-ing a friend in you   to trav-el through the night,

B♭/G   Am/D   Dm
Find-ing a friend in you   who will be there in the morn-ing,

B♭/G   Cm   Dm/C   Cm E♭/C Dm/G
Find-ing a friend in you   to hold me through the night. . . .

Chord Explanations:

Gm9   Dm9   Fmaj7   F6   Am9

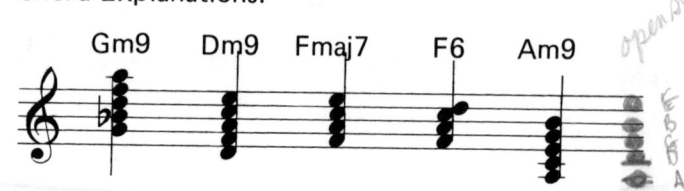

Take It With You Wherever You Go

Words and Music by
HOLLY NEAR

Copyright 1978 Hereford Music

Warnings

Words and Music by
HOLLY NEAR

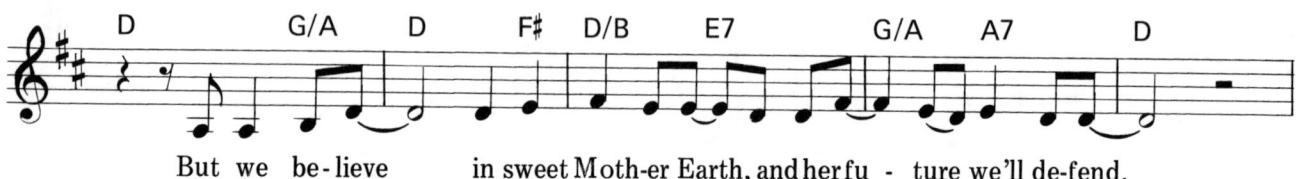

Copyright 1982 Hereford Music

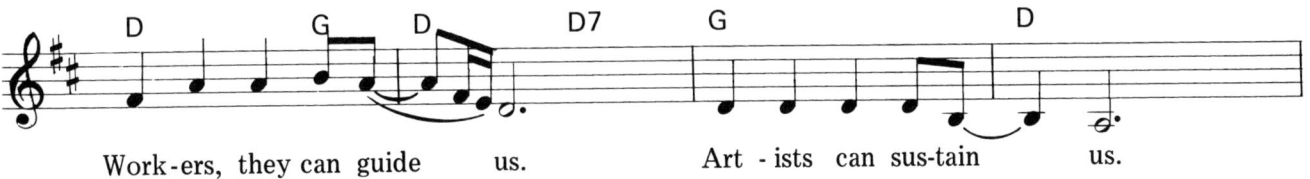
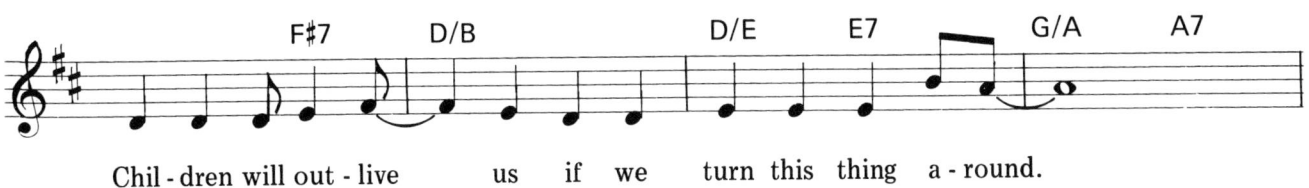

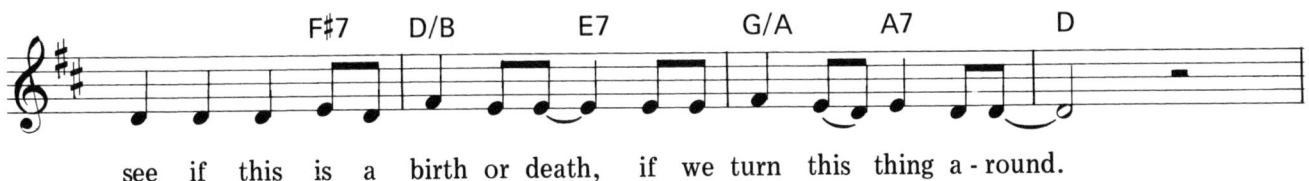
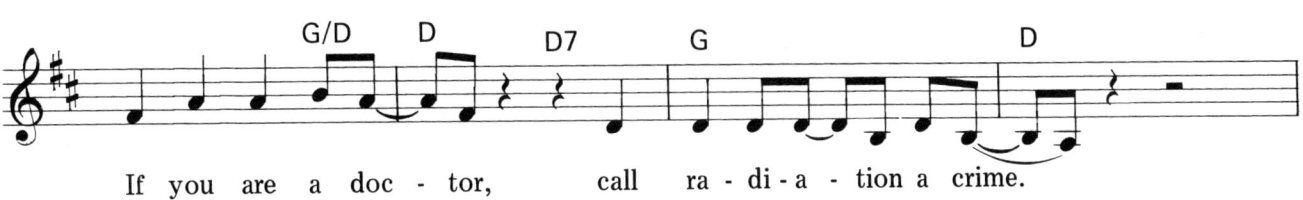
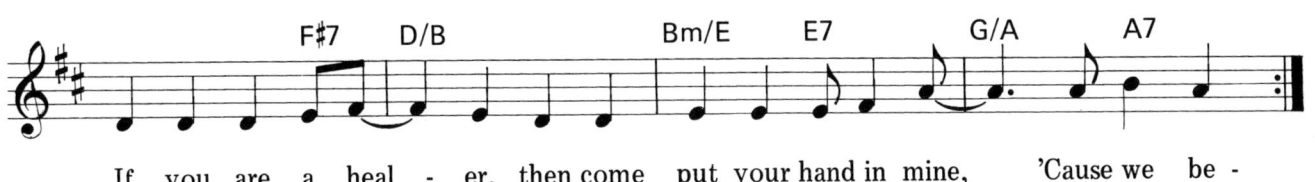

Working Woman

Words and Music by
HOLLY NEAR

I'm a work-ing wom-an, and they call me "Nine to Five."

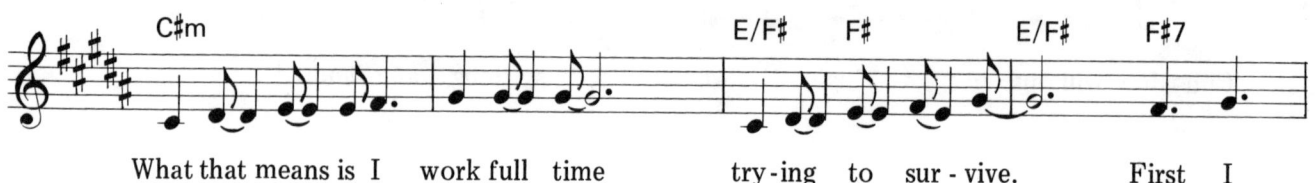
What that means is I work full time try-ing to sur-vive. First I

take care of boss' busi-ness, and then I go home and take care of mine. Oh,

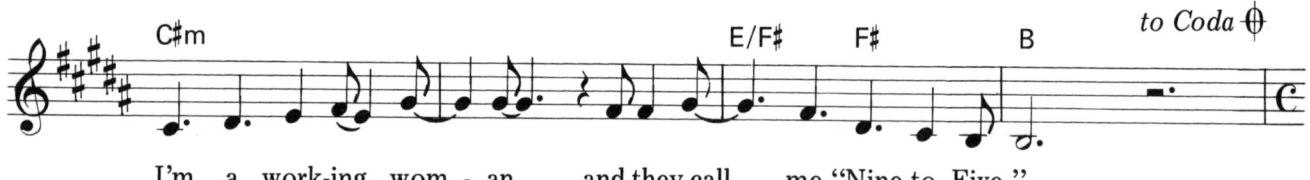
I'm a work-ing wom-an, and they call me "Nine to Five."

File a lot, smile a lot. "Yes, sir. Have a good day!"

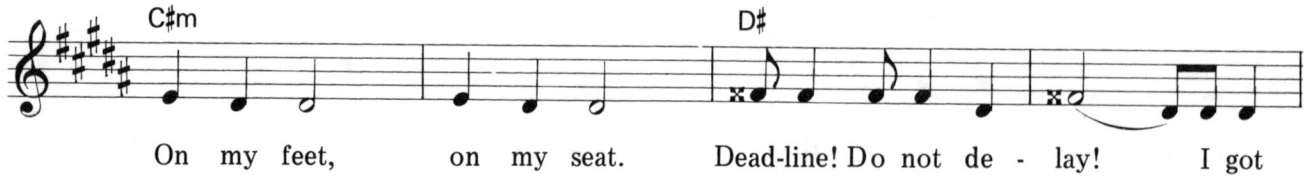
On my feet, on my seat. Dead-line! Do not de-lay! I got

Copyright 1981 Hereford Music

Wrap The Sun Around You

Words and Music by
HOLLY NEAR

Copyright 1981 Hereford Music

"Some accompanists who've interpreted my music."

JEFF LANGLEY

J.T. THOMAS

HOLLY, MARY WATKINS

Notes:

Notes: